EASTWARD BOUND

Cover design by Patricia Probert Gott
Layout and effects by Laura Wiley Ashton
www.gitflorida.com

You may contact her at www.prgottbooks.net

This book is non-fiction.

ISBN 978-0-9845898-1-4

Published by **PRGott Books**
P.O.Box 43, Norway, ME, 04268

Printed in the United States of America

To my grandparents, Annie and Henry Kenoyer
and their ten children, Jean, Joe, Win, Helen, Alice,
Bob, Ruth, John, Russell, and Martha

CONTENTS

EASTWARD BOUND

Annie and Henry Kenoyer-1953

By **PATRICIA PROBERT GOTT**

As CONVEYED by HER AUNT
RUTH KENOYER POLLEY

Published by PRGott Books
P O Box 43, Norway, Maine 04268
www.prgottbooks.net

CHAPTER ONE

Kenoyer Family Dynamics

When I came into the world June 29, 1920 in the very small town of Houghton Iowa, my family consisted of my Mom and Pop, four brothers, and two sisters. Jean Ellis was the oldest, born in 1911, followed closely by Joseph Cartland, 1912; Winfred Arthur, 1914; Helen Esther, 1915; Alice Marie, 1917; and Robert Evert, 1919. Three more siblings would soon follow me, Ruth Elizabeth. They were John Henry, 1922; Russell Edward, 1923; and lastly, Martha Sue born in 1927.

When we were growing up in the West, we were a migrant family that moved wherever there was work for Pop. Our family had moved twenty-six times before traveling east to Maine.—see Addendum B. Pop worked at whatever job, (mostly on farms or ranches handling horses) wherever he could, to put food on our table. Sometimes food was scarce, luxuries were non-existent, but love was abundant.

Just before moving to Iowa, my family had lived in South Dakota where my Pop worked at the Boling Ranch and Mom taught school on the Lower Brule Indian Reservation. My older siblings befriended a particular Indian family that reciprocated by bestowing them with Indian names: Joe was "Don't Eat Dog," Win was "Short Jumper," Alice was "Feather Blew over the Mountain," and Helen was "Long Lady Drippy Nose."

My oldest brother Jean was the sociable one, always helpful and tenderhearted. Joe was quiet, neat, and scholarly. I was intimidated by Win and although I admired his cleverness, he was apt to be sarcastic and sometimes his words hurt me. Helen was a natural born leader, always my older sister. Alice was smart and a book worm; in later years we were very close. Bob was bold, bossy, and lucky. John was precocious and fun loving. I loved Russell very much; he and I were the closest. Martha was my "charge"; it was my job to look after her. . . I felt like I almost raised her. I was the caretaker.

Mom, Annie Berry Kenoyer, born in Lewiston, Maine on January 29, 1884, stood barely five-feet tall, but her persona was huge. She was definitely the head of our family: energetic, non-nonsense, thrifty, independent, loving, and, disciplinarian. When she was a small child her mother, Susan Cartland Berry (my grandmother), moved her family from Maine to Rhode Island where she was a Quaker minister to several parishes. The Berry family eventually moved west to Iowa for health reasons, where Mom graduated from William Penn University (a Quaker college) and began teaching, first in Iowa then in South Dakota. She ran our household like she taught school—organized—delegating tasks and responsibilities to the older children, expecting them to look after and teach those that were younger.

Mom was very capable and a hard worker. She sewed most all our clothes and didn't have a washing machine until Martha, the last child, was born, having to use a wash board and tub before then. She was also very knowledgeable, and being a teacher, helped us with our studies as well as teaching us responsibility, morals, and about life in general.

And her cooking was exceptional! Not only would we *never* have been allowed to waste food by being fussy and not eating, we ate everything she cooked with gusto. I especially loved her pumpkin pies that had a taste like no one else's; and her crusts were never soggy. I liked her pancakes, too, cooked on her unique, three-burner grill, very quick and handy to feed so many mouths. Her rare grill became coveted by many friends and relatives. Eventually, it was passed down to Win's wife, Muriel, so it stayed in the family.

During rainy or cold-wintry days Mom made taffy candy for us to "pull". We even had "taffy-pulling" parties to entertain ourselves. It was so much fun, and of course we ended up eating most of it when it got cold and firmly set.

Mom baked bread every Saturday so we ate homemade bread for lunch sandwiches. At the same time, she would deep-fry bread dough pieces—called squaw bread—which were utterly delicious.

When she made donuts, which was often, I would sneak through the kitchen and grab a couple of donut centers and eat the dough raw. I guess my other siblings did the same because years later, Mom said she knew what we were all doing and had made enough dough to allow for the missing "centers". She was a dear. I could praise Mom for a long time and not run out of good things to say.

On the other hand, Pop, Henry Evert Kenoyer, born September 4, 1884, was her antithesis: over six-feet tall, slender, laid back, happy-go-lucky, loved everyone and every thing. His talents ran to farming and animals, horses especially, and cattle, as he'd been born in Nebraska and was a cowboy when Mom met him. Later, goats, chickens, and pigs were added to his repertoire.

CHAPTER TWO

Living in Iowa

My earliest memory is living in West Point, Iowa, next to neighbors named Johnson. My brothers told me that on their farm they had a great big pig, called a sow, which was soooooo BIG that I couldn't even imagine it. So, of course, I made a special visit to the sow, and it *was* all they said, and more. I was astounded and have never forgotten her size. She also had piglets which had to be removed from their mother so she wouldn't roll on them and smother them.

I was always small for my age. Mom would tell people that when I began walking, I was so short I could walk upright under a dining room table and never touch the top. I also felt very shy. My mother used to encourage me to visit two older lady-friends of hers, Mrs. Bean and Mrs. Farrar, for an afternoon once in a while, which she hoped would teach me to be more outgoing, as well getting me off her hands for a while.

This particular day I was playing under their table. It was constructed with a large center support with lion-shaped feet on the floor, where I sat hidden away quiet like a mouse. While I was under there, I kept my eye on what was happening around me and I suddenly spied some hot dogs in a paper wrapper where one of the ladies had laid them on chair. I quickly reached over, took one, and ate it. In a little while Mrs. Bean discovered one less hot dog. When asked, I confessed that I had eaten it, and she became very excited and concerned. She said that it might kill me, which didn't really scare me because I knew I had eaten raw hot dogs before at home when Mom wasn't looking. I felt very special because she cared so much. We ate *cooked* hot dogs for supper that evening, and all was well. When my mother came for me, Mrs. Bean immediately told her what happened. Mom just laughed and said "Don't be upset; Ruth's eaten raw dogs before and it hasn't done her any harm."

Also impressed into my memory around this time, is going to school. I felt very small being in a classroom with older kids. I was timid and shy at first but I loved my teacher. In general, I grew to like all my subjects, except history, and I got good grades even through high school, making straight A's most all of the time.

The last place where we lived in Iowa was Keokuk, a small mill town. My father was employed at the DuPont Powder Works which produced black gunpowder. It was a dirty job. Every night when Pop came home from work he was covered with fine black dust like miners who worked underground. Mom made him wash up before he came into the house. The pay was above average, but the job was dangerous. Frequent explosions occurred: some minor, injuring a single man, some major, causing several workers at a time to be sent home with severe burns. Once in a while an explosion would cause a worker to die, and sadly all the families in town would attend his funeral. The worker's family would have to move in with relatives, if they had any.

The village had been established for the mill workers and it was laid out precisely like a "T" with one wide main street down the middle (this is where we lived) and the other street ran across the top forming the T. There was also a narrow street, more like an alley, that ran in back of our house.

Houses that lined the streets, like ours, were very modestly built and not really big enough for all nine of us, but we managed anyhow, sleeping several to a bed in three bedrooms. My parents slept in one, the boys in another, and we girls in the third; plus, there was a kitchen. The backyard held a sandbox, a small play area, and our water pump. There was a small barn, more like a shed, and, of course, an outhouse—no indoor plumbing. We had to carry and heat water to wash dishes, wash clothes, and for the tub when we took our Saturday night bathes. A wooden fence bordered our backyard; in fact, each yard was fenced in. I guess the management felt that good fences made good neighbors.

By this time my family had grown to six boys, three girls, plus Mom and Pop. Then in June 1927, a couple of weeks after the beginning summer school vacation, my youngest sister, Martha Sue, was born. We children were sent to the neighbors to keep out from under foot for the day. Fortunately, she slept in a crib in my parents' room as the other two bedrooms were already full with us nine kids.

We were quite happy here, at least we kids were. There were lots of other children in this town, and we all found and made friends with others our age. I especially remember two girls I played with. One was a very light-haired blonde girl my age and size, named Leona. We played together most every day and had great adventures. She lived on the other side of the main street where there was a town dump up beyond her house. We used to frequent there where we found bottles, dishes, pans, and some old furniture which we'd used to make a playhouse in the nearby woods. These woods didn't belong to us, but no one seemed to mind.

Leona and I had another connection to this dump as the trash collector had a white horse and wagon in which he gathered the trash from the back of each house. My friend and I firmly believed that if we saw a white horse and stamped it one hundred times, our wish would come true. To "stamp" a horse, one must lap the thumb, press it into the palm of your other hand, then hit that palm with one's fist . . . thus it's stamped. As many times as we could see the white horse, we could stamp it. So we would run through the town in order to see him again, and although our wishes were not answered, we never gave up.

My other friend was of German descent, named Edna, and she was what they called "tongue-tied". It was hard to understand her speech, but I learned and could even talk like her—much to my siblings' chagrin.

One day Edna and her mother asked me to stay for dinner with them. I ran home to get permission from my mother than back to my friend's home again. The food was not memorable; but I *was* surprised when we were served *beer,* which I drank as did the rest of the family. Of course, this being a novel event for me, I delighted in telling Mom that I had drank some beer. She adamantly told me I must not drink it again. That was just the way it was! We were raised Quaker and alcohol was forbidden.

My brother Bob, who was a year older than me, liked to wander and go exploring alone. Mom would scold him every time he came home because he hadn't told her he was going off. One of these times, when he was seven years old, he'd heard there was a circus in the next town, eight to ten miles away. Again, telling no one, he left early in the morning and was gone all day. When he came home that night, we asked him what he'd seen at the circus. He replied, "Elephants."

Apparently, he'd gotten a job watering the elephants and that was all he saw at the circus.

But he came home with some cash and was happy about that. For years afterward, the family teased him about "seeing circus elephants." I felt sorry for him at the time; it was such a long way to walk, and then he'd had to work instead of seeing the circus. But I secretly thought he was very brave and envied his adventure.

The town's population was no more two hundred people. A brook ran at the base of a small hill at the edge of town where another small settlement lay. We got to know some of the children there and played with them, especially around the crick.

* * * * * * * * *

As a rule this area in Iowa got very little snow, but when it did, we kids took advantage of it and went sledding down the small hill, which was also the main road. There were usually very few cars or horses to look out for. But one day my oldest brother, Jean, started down the hill just as a car came up behind us. Our lookout, Joe, hollered at him, to pull over and let the car pass. Jean guided his sled off the road, but unfortunately, when he did, he struck a fence post—smack. He asked our brother Win to help him, but Win refused because he didn't believe Jean was hurt . . . thought he was just faking it as my brothers sometimes did just kidding around. But Jean wasn't faking; he couldn't get up onto his feet. So we flagged down the next car that came along and asked the driver to give Jean a ride back to our house.

When he got home, Mom found his right leg was ripped open in the groin area. After binding up Jean's leg to give it support and to stop the bleeding, Mom drove him to the hospital in the next town of Summerville. The doctor put six stitches in his leg and wanted him to stay overnight, but Mom, needing to keep down the cost, convinced the doctor to let her take Jean home. The hospital staff was very cooperative and tried to tell her how to care for the wound; but accidents, cuts, and sprains were not unusual for a family of twelve, and my mother told them she knew what to do. As the wound healed, Mom pulled out the stitches herself—no infection developed.

This mishap took away our sledding fun for a time, but we had other things to do as snow in Iowa didn't last long anyway; the climate was too warm.

In the center of our settlement there was a large grassy area where the boys played games like baseball or kickball and we girls played hop-scotch. We all joined in playing Hide & Go Seek; our version of this we called "Beacon, Beacon" because once you were found you could go hide again if someone gave you a signal or "beacon". This center was lighted at night, and we often wished to play outside after dark but our school-night curfew was eight o'clock. We hated having to go to bed when we could hear the other children still playing.

In the summertime our curfew was nine o'clock, and we could stay outside playing longer. We often played in the tall cornfields. I was still pretty small and just a little fearful of getting lost as the corn stalks were high over my head. I wouldn't venture very deep into the corn. My older brothers and sisters, however, had a grand old time. I still get a warm-fuzzy feeling when recalling fond memories of the corn fields in Iowa.

Iowa Cornfields

CHAPTER THREE

Preparing to Travel

We had exceptional parents, but our financial circumstances were not the best: the powder mill was not a safe place for a man with ten children to work. But money was still tight, as were our accommodations. We lived very cramped in our house and yard. My parents were concerned, but they didn't talk of this in front of us children. We'd hear their solemn talk after we were in bed at night. Although their words were muffled, we knew something was in the offing.

My grandmother, Susan Cartland Berry, had written my mother over the past year, urging her and family to come live in Maine, especially to escape Pop's dangerous job. My Grandmother Berry was very concerned and she promised to have a house or farm large enough for us all to live in comfortably and would help us financially. There had been a recent explosion where a co-worker of my father's had died, which might have prompted my parents to seriously consider her offer. Mom and Pop thought about this for some time before telling us about their decision to move east.

When they finally told us children that we would be moving away to Maine, the news spread like wild fire because we each told our friends, who spread the word to *their* families and friends. All the neighbors were excited for us, and many showed they were sorry to see us go. This was especially true of the lady next door, Mrs. Horner, who shed tears and told mom, "I don't know how I'll get along without your friendship," even though she had several children to keep her company. She had said she envied Mom's ability to organize and get things done, along with raising ten children as well as she did.

In the ensuing weeks we children were told many tales about Maine. How there would be lots of ferocious animals like bears and moose nearby, some wild Indians living there, much dark and foggy weather, and with long snowy winters—we liked the sound of that! I was told you wouldn't be able to wave to someone at a distance because they wouldn't see you due to the ever present thick fog or snow. We were warned that it would be a longgggggg, longgggggg trip, but that meant little to me. I didn't have much of an idea where *Maine* was, much less any concept of distance.

* * *   * * *   * * *

In getting ready to travel Mom told each of us that we could take *one* favorite thing or toy with us. We had to clear it with her first because there was not any extra room in the vehicles we'd be traveling in—a 1920s Dodge touring car

and a Model-T Ford pickup truck.

So I asked myself, *what shall I take?* Then I remembered a little flowered sauce dish that I had earned by learning the books of the Bible in Sunday school at the Episcopal Church. We were Quakers (so Mom said) but this was the only church available to us, and since there was no Quaker Meeting House or Quaker Church around, Mom felt her children should go to church even though it was not our faith.

When I showed my dish to Mom, she said it would go in with the dishes we were taking anyway, so it was okay. The dishes, including my dish, would be packed in a barrel to go in the truck body. I made sure my special dish was wrapped securely in my sweater so that it wouldn't get broken. It was my treasured memento.

In the meantime my friend, Leona, gave me a goodbye gift. It was a cupid doll on a stick shaped like a cane. It had soft feathers and colorful ribbons, and I thought it was pretty special. Her brother had played for it at a carnival and won it as a game prize. I planned to take it with me on my long trip to Maine. It would take up no room as I would hold it.

Helen packed a small box of pictures and cards she'd collected. Alice brought her favorite book she had won in a reading contest. Bob brought a piece of rope to practice tying knots with, John brought a wooden toy boat someone had carved for him, Russell brought his special rag-toy animal, and Martha, well she was just a year old and didn't know what was happening.

A large gathering of friends and neighbors met at out house to see us off. Everyone was excited, some were crying, some were worried, and many were doubtful that this was the right thing to do—to move so far away.

Someone had a camera and took pictures of our family eating watermelon. As the shutter clicked, we were up to our ears in sweet melon, thinking maybe this would be our last meal until reaching Maine—what did we know, we were just excited kids liking all the attention.

My folks had planned well how all twelve of us were going to fit into the one car and one truck. The pickup carried the bulky wooden barrel packed with pots, pans, metal dishes and glassware wrapped in our clothes with blankets stacked and secured on top. Another contained a few more clothes, towels, and more blankets top. Two more boxes held the bread and muffins Mom had been making ahead for the trip, some dried beans, grains, and fruit that would ripen during the trip donated by friends. And, Mom refused to leave her Maytag washer, so that was on board also, strapped securely into a corner behind the cab.

Three persons would ride in the front seat of the truck: Pop, Win and Jean, who was sixteen and would relieve Pop's driving when he got tired. All the rest of us were to travel in the Dodge touring car since it was large and we children were quite small, except Joe, who, although he didn't have a driver's license, would help Mom drive. Bob, John, and Russell sat in the middle seat. Helen, Alice, Martha Sue, and I fit in the back seat but without much moving space—I got to sit by the window. Helen and Alice took turns holding baby Martha on their laps when Mom was driving. The hard part was that Martha was a little over a year old and in the process of being potty trained, so a small potty was in the car with us—this would prove awkward to accomplish while driving across the country for ten days in tight quarters.

August 26, 1928 began as a clear day; bright cloudless skies foretold a good start to our journey. After many hugs, kisses, and promises to write, we drove off.

CHAPTER FOUR

Maine, Here We Come

Although we were now on our way, I didn't have much insight into how far away Maine was, nor how we were going to get there. I held my cupid doll on a cane in my hand. My older brother Joe said, "You'd better not stick that out the car window," but he didn't tell me why. I found out a little while later, when, as we were moving slowly through the next town, I *did* stick it out the open car window, and just as quick, it was gone into the wind. But it was our first day of travel and I was too excited to cry.

Before the day's end we came to the "Great" Mississippi River, that's what Mom called it. We drove onto a barge that ferried us across. This was very exciting as it seemed miles to the other side, and I had never been on a boat or seen such a large river. I thought it was as big as an ocean. I re-named it the Great "Big" Mississippi River.

As we left Iowa, we sang our rendition of "Maine or Bust".

On the second day of driving through the flat land of Illinois toward Chicago, with Pop leading in the truck and Mom following in the Dodge, a train whistle blew in the distance—we all thought. Neither Mom nor Pop had seen the train and had no idea it was coming so fast. The truck drove across some railroad tracks, but the "Yankee Flyer" train was traveling fast-fast, and our car, containing all of us kids, just barely made it over the tracks when the train shot past our rear, going like a bullet. We were all terrified but, thankfully, okay.

My brothers said: "Golly, I bet that it was going at least a hundred miles an hour."

"I never saw the likes of that."

"Wow! That could have been the end of us."

None of us ever forgot that close call.

The first day had been exciting crossing the Mississippi and beginning a new adventure. The second day had also proved adventurous almost being run down by a train. By the end of the third day I was getting a little bored, except I didn't dare say so. By the fourth day we invented road games of who could count the most cows, horses, cars, trucks. Helen paired up to help Russell, and Alice paired up with John. Bob and I could hold our own in the counting games and sometimes even beat my older sisters as we tried harder.

We also sang to entertain ourselves. Old favorites that we all knew: "She'll be Coming 'Round the Mountain", "Oh Susanna" and "Darling Clementine". When we ran out of those, we'd sing church hymns: "Jesus Loves Me", "Old Rugged Cross" and "Church in the Wildwood". We'd proceed to see who could sing the loudest, until we would end up yelling; at that point, Mom would tell us to quit.

In the early evenings we always stopped driving and found a field or clearing to get off the highway to camp for the night that had fresh water nearby to drink and use for cooking. That gave us younger children time to explore around to see what we could discover. One evening we camped near a fairgrounds where my brother Bob (known to be lucky) went exploring and found quite a bit of change around the grounds—as much as a dollar in coins. He was proud of his find; we were happy for him.

Mom cooked supper, mostly beans or tomato soup, over a two-burner Colman gas camp stove. We stopped frequently along the way to pick tomatoes, as farmers said we could have them for FREE if we picked them ourselves. We all got very tired of eating tomato soup, but no one complained. We were hungry. Breakfast was cornmeal mush, which I disliked but ate it anyway, or oatmeal, no sugar, just a bit milk added, which I liked better. Lunch was bananas and muffins. Mom's muffins were extra good and she made them a lot; Pop made them sometimes too. We were a muffin-loving family.

At dusk, the older boys, Jean, Joe and Win would dig out the blankets and distribute (throw) them to us to roll up in to sleep. Baby Martha was wrapped up tightly and placed between Mom and Pop so she couldn't get up and wander away. We kept our clothes on for added warmth and in case we awoke and had to go potty during the night. Potty privacy was easier at night. Sometimes if we had to "go" during the day and there were no bushes around, it was boys on the left side, girls on the right.

One night Pop woke us all up as a heavy thunder storm was developing. We could see flashes of lightening, and the thunder was beginning to boom loudly. He knew we would soon need to get out of the rain or get drenched. As it happened, we'd camped near a building with a large porch, so as Mom gathered Martha in her arms, Pop hustled the rest of us into the building where we slept, wrapped in our blankets, the rest of the night. In the morning we found that the building was a dance hall. The man who owned it came around and told my Pop that he was glad we'd made use of it " . . . or you'd have been soaked to the skin," he said.

When we arrived in Detroit, Michigan, our route took us into Canada, around the north side of Lake Erie. After five days of traveling, playing road games, singing all the songs we knew, and not sleeping too well on the ground because of being eaten by night bugs, we all became tired and took naps throughout the day. Mom would say, "Wake up. This is an important place and you'll want to remember it." I'd sometimes open my eyes and manage to stay awake, sometimes not.

I was *very* awake when we came back across the Canadian/United States border into Niagara, New York. We presented quite a crew to be inspected at the custom station. The border authorities signaled Joe to stop and he had to push the brake clear to the floor because the brakes were worn so badly. We finally stopped in the middle of the crossing. This seemed to irritate one guard as he came striding up to the window wearing a frown. I was a little frightened and slouched in the backseat corner. He then questioned whether Joe should be driving. The guard said, "You don't look big enough to drive." I think he meant "old" enough, but that's not what he said.

Mom jumped out of the car, all five foot one of her, hands on her hips, and said to the guard, "And just how *big* does one have to be to drive? I drive most all the time and my son's much *bigger* than me."

Joe, although only fifteen years old, stood near six feet, hung his head, trying to look contrite, hiding a smirk.

Taken back by Mom's feisty manner, the guard looked down at her, shook his head, and chuckled. Mom then explained that she was always next to her son when he drove, and that he was a big help to her when she needed to rest a spell. He must have found our faces honest and our plight in need of compassion and understanding because we were allowed to pass.

As we drove by the other officials that had been inspecting our car and truck, they saw so many faces that one officer smiled and asked Pop, "You sure you got 'em all?" and waved us on.

On the American side of Niagara Falls,

we stopped to see the rushing river and powerful waterfalls. The falls were surrounded by mist and fog and I couldn't see bottom, maybe there wasn't a bottom . . . an abyss, that's what Helen called it.

We also visited a Kellogg's Shredded Wheat factory in the area where we were given shredded wheat biscuits for FREE. We joyfully ate many of these with a banana sliced on the top. Either I was awfully hungry, or they tasted real good—maybe both. Unbeknown to the family, Mom and Pop were concerned that we were running low on food at this time and we still had a ways to go before arriving in Maine. They prayed a lot.

* * *   * * *   * * *

My parents said that: we were now in New England (wherever that was) and were nearing Maine (which sounded good), but first we needed to get through and over the lower Berkshire Mountains of Massachusetts. Of course I didn't know what that meant at the time, but soon learned as we had trouble getting the vehicles up the steep mountain grades. In fact, one was so steep that the Ford truck had to *back* up the mountain because it didn't have enough power to make it over the top going frontward. And the hairpin turns were enough to scare me to death. I'll never forget looking out the window and seeing nothing but tree tops below. I didn't look out again. I couldn't wait to get to Maine.

We traveled through Boston, ". . . several times," as Pop would later tell others, "until we found the highway heading north again."

On September 4th, 1928, twelve Kenoyers crossed the bridge into Kittery, Maine with whoops and hollers from my brothers and squeals of delight from us girls. My folks didn't say much as they were pretty conservative, but we could sense their relief as we neared the end of our journey.

As we drove along the coast of Maine, I caught glimpses of the ocean. I was wide awake now! Where the water met the land was very rocky, and there were big waves splashing against ledges. I began daydreaming and wondering how far it was to land again once one started sailing across the ocean, and if there were giant sea creatures hidden beneath. Then we left the coast and began to drive inland where trees were everywhere, maybe sheltering the bear, moose, and Indians I'd been warned about.

We drove as far as Lewiston where my mother's cousin, Dora Page, lived. She had said she would take us in whenever we arrived—and here we were. Dora (we called her Aunt Dora) was a pretty lady, plump and short, who kissed and hugged, and kissed us all again. Her house was small but she found areas for us to sleep on the floor, and it was better than the ground we'd been sleeping on for the past ten days. She fed us and made us feel welcome to Maine, our new state.

* * * * * * * * *

Maine Countryside

Later I learned that gas had cost ten cents per gallon, and we had traveled at least 1400 miles. Besides purchasing gas, my parents had also known they would have to buy fresh milk from farmers along the way and a few other food stuffs, but the trip turned out more expensive than they'd planned. Pop arrived in Maine with just twenty-five cents left in his pocket, the gas gauges were on empty, and the only food that remained were a few bananas, which we ate the morning before we arrived at Aunt Dora's.

EPILOGUE

Our family expanded in 1931 when Cousin Charles (Chuck) Sisson, 11 years old (same age as me) came to live with us and was adopted into our midst. His mother had contracted scarlet fever and died, and his father was not able to take care of him. From the time he came to live with us, Chuck was treated as our brother. He brought merriment and a comic personality. He and John were close and often entertained the family with their comedy acts and impressions.

We lived in four different homes before finally settling onto a hundred acres in Windsor, Maine in 1935, in what we named the Yellow Box Ranch because it was painted yellow and looked like a box. There were two bedrooms downstairs, plus a kitchen, a combination dining and living room, and a parlor. Two small bedrooms and an open attic were upstairs. A sun porch was added in later years and indoor plumbing was eventually installed. There was a large livestock barn, hog sheds, hen houses, and a garage. Pop happily farmed, raising cattle, goats, chickens, pigs, and owned a horse or two for a time. Mom taught at a nearby school in Windsor, teaching nearly into her seventies. Martha, Russell, John, Bob, Alice and I all had her for a teacher at that school. The Yellow Box Ranch would remain their home until Pop died in 1966 and Mom in 1972.

Unfortunately, my youngest brother Russell was killed in 1945 during WWII, flying for the Air Force.

* * * * * * * * *

By the 1960s our extended family became fifty-six, with spouses and the arrival of all my thirty-five nieces and nephews.—see Addendum A. The next generation, in the 1980s, brought the total to one hundred and fifty, and with the turn of the century, at least two hundred seventy-five descendants of the original ten Kenoyers could be accounted for.

Addendum A

TEN KEYOYERS & THEIR CHILDREN

JEAN AND PEG
- James
- Paul
- Judith
- Nancy
- Christopher

JOE AND VAN
- Joseph Jr.
- Elaine
- Susan

WIN AND MURIEL
- Ronald
- Karen
- Suzanne
- Scott

HELEN AND CHARLES
- Richard
- Margaret
- Winifred
- David

ALICE AND TOBY
- Gordon
- Patricia
- Russell
- Randall
- Rebecca
- David

BOB AND BEV
- Donald
- George
- Steven

RUTH AND LELAND
- None

JOHN AND SHIRLEY
- Janet
- Galen
- Marilyn
- Christopher

MARTHA AND ELLIOT
- Sandra
- Robert
- Gerald
- Kathryn
- Douglas
- Jennifer

RUSSELL
- None

Addendum B

PLACES MOM & POP CALLED HOME
IN SOUTH DAKOTA & IOWA

1911-1912 – Homestead, Vale, SD
                            – Jean's birthplace

1912 – Erie house, Vale, SD – summer only

1912 – Mother's ranch, Vale, SD
              – fall and winter – Joe born here

1913 – Uncle Steven's ranch, Vale, SD
                        – spring and summer

1914 – Homestead rebuilt, Vale, SD
                        – Winfred's birthplace

1915 – Eaton house, Vale, SD
         – summer and fall – Helen's birthplace

1915-1916 – Town of Vale, SD – winter only

1916 – Johnson Ranch, between Vale and
                    Sturgis, SD – one year

1917 – On farm toward Sturgis, SD
                    – two weeks in spring

1917 – Mitchell house, Sturgis, SD
                    – two months in spring

1917 – Kaubish Ranch, Sturgis, SD
                    – spring and summer

1917 – Mitchell house, Sturgis, SD
                    – Alice's birthplace

1917 – Chilli Restaurant, Sturgis, SD
                    – fall through December

1918 – Upstairs Apt. Sturgis, SD
                    – two weeks

1918 – Berriman House, Sturgis, SD
             – winter, rooming house – spring

1918 – Boveen Ranch, north of Sturgis
             Bare Butte Valley, SD – summer

1918 – Boling Ranch, Lower Brule, SD – fall

1919 – George Smith house, Lower Brule, SD
                    – Bob's birthplace

1919 – Next door to George Smith house,
                    Lower Brule, SD

1920 – Indian Log House, Lower Brule, SD
                              – two months spring

1920 – White's Institute Farm, Houghton, IA
                              – Ruth's birthplace

1921 – Another school farm, Houghton, IA
                                    – spring

1921, 22, 23 – Steffenmeier's farm,
              West Point, IA – John's birthplace

1923, 24, 25 – Neff's farm, Donnelson, IA
                              – Russell's birthplace

1926 – Hentzel farm, New Boston, IA
                              – spring and summer

1926, 27, 28 – Powder Works housing,
              Keokuk, IA – Martha's birthplace

Kenoyer children in Iowa, 1924
John, Ruth, Bob, Alice, Helen, Win, Joe, Jean and Russell

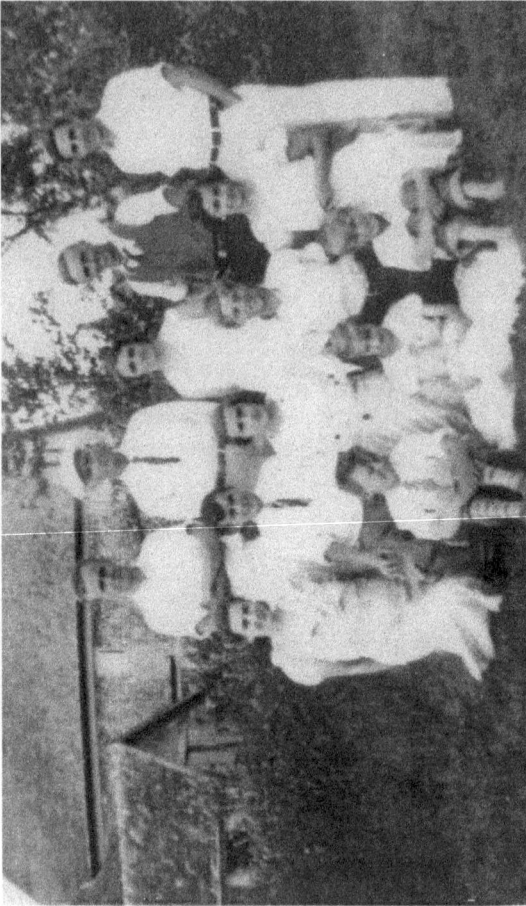

Kenoyers in Maine, 1934 - Jean, Pop, Mom, Joe, Win Helen, Bob, Ruth, John, Alice Cousin Chuck, Martha, and Russell

Kenoyers, 1961 - Ruth, Bob, Alice, John, Martha, Win, Helen
Jean, Pop, Mom, Joe

ACKNOWLEDGMENTS

My Aunt Ruth Kenoyer Polley was instrumental in documenting and relating the facts for this book. Although my mom, Alice Kenoyer Probert, recounted a few of the Kenoyer clan's early tales and adventures and their way of life to me while I was growing up, I told her stories in the book from my Aunt Ruth's perspective.

Many thanks to Aunt Helen Kenoyer Mosher who lent her memory when Aunt Ruth and I became stumped with dates and details of life in Iowa and South Dakota, and for supplying information on my Grandmother Kenoyer's family background. She is the Grande Dame of the family.

It was important to show the strength, courage, and unity this family demonstrated as they persevered throughout the children's early childhood with hard work, integrity and love. The siblings went on to become loving spouses, successful parents, and hard workers all, from a white-collar business owner to a solid blue-collar worker, a school teacher, FBI agent, school principal, church pastor, registered nurse, and chemist. We of the third and succeeding generations are very proud of them.

Patricia Probert Gott